POETRY

A Day for Anne Frank

Lies

I Am the Bitter Name

The Lark. The Thrush.
The Starling. (Poems
from Issa)

With Ignorance

Tar

Flesh and Blood

Poems 1963–1983

Helen

A Dream of Mind

Selected Poems

The Vigil

Repair

Love About Love

The Singing

Collected Poems

Creatures

Wait

ESSAYS

Poetry and Consciousness

On Whitman

In Time: Poets,
Poems, and the Rest

MEMOIR

Misgivings

TRANSLATIONS

Sophocles' Women of Trachis
(with Gregory Dickerson)

The Bacchae of Euripides

Canvas, by Adam Zagajewski
(translated with Renata
Gorczynski and Benjamin Ivry)

Selected Poems of Francis Ponge
(with John Montague and
Margaret Guiton)

WRITERS WRITING DYING

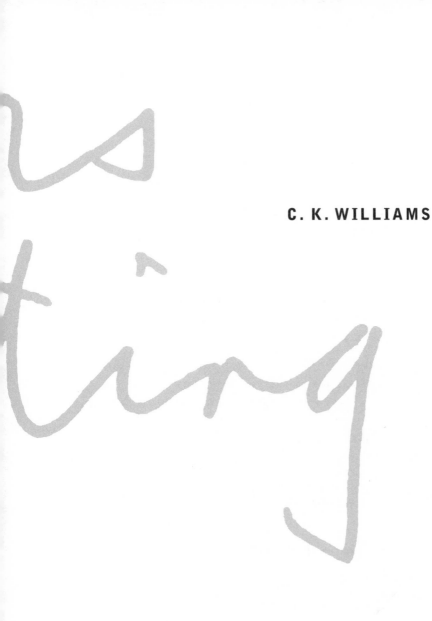

C. K. WILLIAMS

FARRAR STRAUS GIROUX

NEW YORK

FARRAR, STRAUS AND GIROUX

18 WEST 18TH STREET, NEW YORK 10011

COPYRIGHT © 2012 BY C. K. WILLIAMS

ALL RIGHTS RESERVED

DISTRIBUTED IN CANADA BY D&M PUBLISHERS, INC.

PRINTED IN THE UNITED STATES OF AMERICA

FIRST EDITION, 2012

LIBRARY OF CONGRESS CATALOGING-IN-PUBLICATION DATA

WILLIAMS, C. K. (CHARLES KENNETH), 1936–

   WRITERS WRITING DYING / C. K. WILLIAMS. — 1ST ED.

    P. CM.

   ISBN 978-0-374-29332-1 (ALK. PAPER)

   I. TITLE.

 PS3573.I4483 W75 2012

 811'.54 — DC23

                              2012008048

DESIGNED BY QUEMADURA

WWW.FSGBOOKS.COM

10 9 8 7 6 5 4 3 2

CONTENTS

WRITERS WRITING DYING

WHACKED

Every morning of my life I sit at my desk getting whacked by some great poet
or other.

Some Yeats, some Auden, some Herbert or Larkin, and lately a whole tribe of
others—

oi!—younger than me. *Whack!* Wiped out, every day . . . I mean since becom-
ing a poet.

I mean wanting to—one never is, really, a poet. Or I'm not. Not when I'm try-
ing to write,

though then comes a line, maybe another, but still pops up again Yeats, say,
and again *whacked.*

. . . Wait . . . Old brain in my head, I'd forgotten that "whacked" in crime
movies means murdered,

rubbed out, by the mob—little the mob-guys would think that poets could do
it, and who'd believe

that instead of running away you'd find yourself fleeing *towards* them, some
sweet-seeming Bishop

who's saying *so—so—so,* but *whack!* you're stampeding again through her
poems like a mustang,

whacked so hard that you bash the already-broken crown of your head on the
roof of your stall.

. . . What a relief to read for a while some bad poems. Still, I try not to—bad, whackless poems

can hurt you, can say you're all right when you're not, can condone your poet-coward

who compulsively asks if you're all right—*Am I all right?*—not wasting your time—

Am I wasting time?—though you know you are, wasting time, if you're not being *whacked*.

Bad poems let you off that: the confessional mode now: I've read reams, I've written as many.

Meanwhile, this morning, this very moment, I'm thinking of George Herbert composing;

I see him, by himself, in some candlelit chamber unbearably lonely to us but glorious to him,

and he's hunched over, scribbling, scribbling, and the room's filling with poems whacking at me,

and Herbert's not even paying attention as the huge tide of them rises and engulfs me

in warm tangles of musical down as from the breasts of the choiring dawn-tangling larks.

"Lovely enchanting language, sugar-cane . . ." Whack! *"The sweet strains, the lullings . . ."*

Oh whack! Lowell or Keats, Rilke or Wordsworth or Wyatt: whack—fifty years of it,

old racehorse, plug hauling its junk—isn't it time to be put out to pasture?
But, ah, I'd still

if I could lie down like a mare giving birth, arm in my own uterine channel
to tug out another,

one more, only one more, poor damp little poem, then I'll be happy—I prom-
ise, I swear.

A HUNDRED BONES

In this mortal frame of mine, which consists of a hundred bones and nine orifices, there is something, and this something can be called, for lack of a better name, a windswept spirit . . . **BASHO**

And thus the hundred bones of my body plus various apertures plus that thing
   I don't know yet
to call spirit are all aquake with joyous awe at the shriek of the fighter planes
   that from their base
at Port Newark swoop in their practice runs so low over our building that the
   walls tremble.

Wildcats, they're called, Thunderbolts or Corsairs, and they're practicing
   strafing, which in war means
your machine guns are going like mad as you dive down on the enemy sol-
   diers and other bad people,
Nips, Krauts, trying to run out from under your wings, your bullet-pops leap-
   ing after their feet.

It's a new word for us, *strafing*. We learn others, too: *blockbusters*, for instance,
   which means
bombs that smash down your whole block: not our block, some *Nip* block, or
   Nazi—
some gray block in the newsreel. B-24 is the number of my favorite bomber:
   the Liberator.

My best fighter: *Lightning.* The other kind of lightning once crashed on an
    eave of our building
and my mother cried out and swept me up in her arms: *The war is here,* she
    must have thought,
the war has found me. All her life I think she was thinking: *The war is here, the
    war has found me.*

Some words we don't know yet—*gas chamber, napalm*—children our age, in
    nineteen forty-four, say,
say my friend Arnold and I, who're discussing how we'll torture our treacher-
    ous enemy-friends
who've gone off to a ball game without us. They're like enemies, Japs or Nazis:
    so of course torture.

Do children of all places and times speak so passionately and knowledgeably
    about torture?
Our imaginations are small, though, Arnold's and mine. Tear out their nails.
    Burn their eyes.
Drive icicles in their ear so there's no evidence of your having done it except
    they're dead.

Then it was Arnold who died. He was a doctor, out west; he learned to fly
    Piper Cubs,
and flew out to help Navajo women have babies. He'd become a good man.
    Then he was dead.
But right now: victory! V-Day! Clouds like giant ice creams over the evil
    Japanese empire.

Cities are burning. Some Japanese cities aren't even there. *The war is here! The war has found me!*

Japanese poets come later. We don't know we need them until they're already buffing the lens.

Basho. Issa. Buson. Especially Basho: ah, that *windswept spirit*; ah, that hardly there frog.

Atom bomb, though: Basho as shadow burned into asphalt. House torn by mad burning wind.

Poets in coats of straw, burning. What is our *flaw*, we human beings? What is our *error*?

Spikes in your tushy, ice in your brain. That frog invisibly waiting forever to make its leap.

VILE JELLY

I see they're tidying the Texas textbooks again.
Chopping them down to make little minds stay
the right size for the preachers not to be vexed
as they troll for converts, or congregants, or whatever.

Troll. As in "Fish for Men." As in ". . . for Christ."
Here's a fisher: a pre-biblical king on a slab. Captives.
The king with a not-sharp spear is blinding the first,
thrusting then twisting it into the writhing man's eye.

Subtle carvers they were: you see the thrust and twist.
How the hook, the *fish hook*, driven through the lip
of the victim to keep him from inconveniently struggling
and attached to a rope, tugs the lip out from the teeth.

Because the whole state of Texas buys the same book,
the import of their distortions and falsehoods is wide.
The publishers take them into account,
so other states' schoolbooks are dumbed down as well.

Who said: *With my eyes closed, I see more?* Not me.
Who said: *I study not to learn but hoping
what I've learned might not be true?* Not me again.
I stay still. I peek warily out the door of my stove.

That's a story about seeing, not having to see.
A fairy tale with your usual prince, this time in a stove.
It doesn't say why he's there, even after he's saved,
by your usual virgin. The scholars don't explain either.

My theory is he locked himself in, welded the lid,
because of all he could no longer bear to behold.
Texas textbooks, for instance. Chunks of knowledge
extracted like eyes. Discarded. Thrown on a floor.

Evolution, needless to say. Sociology. Jefferson. Deism.
All these complications henceforth won't vex.
They'll be scraped from the mold. No longer be *seen*.
As much is no longer seen in the world as well.

Will the eyes of conscience also be punctured? Spilled?
Vile jelly, it's called in *King Lear*. Vile jelly. *Out*.
"Chips of blank," Dickinson wrote in a war poem.
"Chips of blank in boyish eyes." Is that still in the books?

Is the king on the slab with his spear and rope?
But that was before Christ rose. Into his own stove.
"The noise of mankind," another god groused,
"is too loud, they keep me awake. Rid me of them."

The underling angels began boiling the acid,
but thanks be someone had learned how to write.
An inscription appeared on a roof.
Please, it pled to the prickly deity, *don't*.

And the almighty, yawning after for once a good nap,
decided to let us do it unto ourselves.
Which we're rushing to do. As quick as we can.
By making the mysteries holy and blank.

By chopping eyes from susceptible minds.
Susceptible hearts. Thou vilest jelly.
Herds of children go bleeding into the dark.
Oh, vile. Thou chips of blank. Thou boyish eyes.

BIANCA BURNING

The sexual terror lions are roaring into my ears as I make my way between
their cages
at the Bertram Mills Circus in England in nineteen fifty-seven when I'm
twenty.
The terrible lions have roared for six months and though I don't know it they'll
roar
for six more then be extinguished, leaving only their irksome echo the rest of
my life.

A circus—I'm traveling with a *circus*, an exotic thing to think, and I have a
Bianca—
not the Bianca Bruno Schulz had in his "Spring," an "enchanting" Bianca
whom one
"would notice . . . how with every step light as a dancer she enters her be-
ing . . ."—a Bianca,
rather, who's lush, ardent, and, though only eighteen, more amorously ad-
vanced than I am,

with breasts too beautiful to remember and that other thing farther down
she'll bring
with her every day to my "digs" to roll with me on my bed, while I flail and
despair,

and return with her back through that savage alley, that gauntlet of error and
    terror,
to the "caravan" where her father and mother lived, and where we ate dinner
    together.

Bianca's father is a clown. Not the way I was a clown, a sexual clown, not the
    way
Schulz depicts himself in his drawings as almost a clown, with his rack of
    compulsions—
Bianca's father's a real clown, famous, with different names in different
    countries,
who in the ring in his Chaplinesque costume is hilarious, reckless, conta-
    giously joyful.

Yet Bianca's father like me is possessed by a terror, though no one dares frame
    it that way.
Bianca's mother, you see, has claustrophobia, a terrible case, and it was agreed
that for her to sleep in their cramped trailer would be painful, insupportable
    really,
so Bianca's beautiful mother, lusher even than Bianca, and so young seen
    from here,

younger than my daughter now, would kiss her impassive, pipe-smoking
    husband
and leave in the car that came every night to take her to the circus owner's
    yacht,

and we remnants, we relics, would gloomily sit; Bianca because soon she'd
    have to go
back to her job as a nightclub dancer, and the husband, for obvious reasons,
    and me,

part of the act now, with my rituals of desire and my dread of the lions I'll pass
    again
as I wend the torturous route to my room to wait for Bianca's next visit
    tomorrow,
with her breasts, and that other thing which I could hardly bring myself in
    those days
to call by its name, so fearsome it was, as it was for the tragic and timid Schulz,

who even in his erotic etchings of perfectly formed nudes with Schulz-like
    men
abjectly groveling, crushed, dejected, under their elegant feet, depicts no
    vaginas,
or none not submerged in inkiest shadow, save one, and that sketchy, in-
    consequential,
which surely proves that Schulz knew the firmament of vagina is fathomless,

without measurable dimensions, altering such shape it does have with im-
    patience,
but for which Schulz's Bianca, who "controlled her glamour with pity,"
and whose wisdom was "full of sadness," must by now offer demure con-
    solation,
while mine, my Bianca, struts with top hat and whip across the arena to take
    her bow.

RAT WHEEL, DEMENTIA, MONT SAINT-MICHEL

FOR ALBERT O. HIRSCHMAN

My last god's a theodicy glutton, a good-evil gourmet—
peacock and plague, gene-junk; he gobbles it down.
Poetry, violence; love, war—his stew of honey and thorn.

For instance, thinks theodicy-god: Mont Saint-Michel.
Sheep, sand, steeple honed sharp as a spear. And inside,
a contraption he calls with a chuckle the rat wheel.

Thick timber three meters around, two persons across,
into which prisoners were inserted to trudge, toil,
hoist food for the bishop and monks; fat bishop himself.

The wheel weighs and weighs. You're chained in; you toil.
Then they extract you. Where have your years vanished?
What difference? says theodicy-god. Wheel, toil: what difference?

Theodicy-god has evolved now to both substance and not.
With handy metaphysical blades to slice brain meat from mind.
For in minds should be voidy wings choiring, not selves.

This old scholar, for instance, should have to struggle to speak,
should not remember his words, paragraphs, books:
that garner of full-ripened grain must be hosed clean.

Sometimes as the rat wheel is screaming, theodicy-god
considers whether to say he's sorry: that you can't speak,
can't remember your words, paragraphs, books.

Sorry, so sorry. Blah, his voice thinks instead, blah.
He can't do it. Best hope instead they'll ask him again
as they always do for forgiveness. But what if they don't?

What might have once been a heart feels pity, for itself though,
not the old man with no speech—for him and his only scorn.
Here in my rat wheel, my Mont Saint-Michel, my steeple of scorn.

LONELY CROW

My depression to my relief isn't yet in the Internet age
but still works from notebooks file cards post-its
so when Vivaldi's *Seasons* blossoms from the stereo

it doesn't know how to google junk from my safe-deposit
of failures and funks but blinks herky-jerky like a quasar
suspending albeit accidently the beyond myself miseries

with which it usually inflicts me—you know: war, poverty,
planet murder, power-mad politicians, the insatiable rich—
chomp, crunch, they're eating us up—but as soon as I cut off

go up to my study my woe's back in business—envy, greed,
absurd unquenchable ambition, and still is at my desk—sigh—
where I'm scrounging for poems to shake me out of myself.

Who should I be reading? Let's see. Neruda? No way, too rich.
Lowell and Larkin, good god, we're already in the pits . . .
Maybe the ancient Chinese?—Wang Wei, Tu Fu, Li Po—

the whole team whose neat poem packets once brought solace
but that now forgive me seem off the point: plum blossoms,
boring; drunkenness, blah; nada even for poems in a lake . . .

Curiously unboring though their biographical sketches—
paupers they were zillionaires shits right and left;
comforting they'd be afflicted with madness not unlike ours . . .

I skim anyway through them again, and find, in Tu Fu,
Song *wearing thoughts thin* . . . Wow . . . *Dragon in hibernation*—
Yes, exactly—no dragons sleeping near here but, look,

there's a crow, who with two wing beats and a glide
like that passage in the *Hammerklavier* I call a tango
though it's not crosses the sky and about whom I think,

"Poor, lonely crow," then realize he's not lonely at all,
more likely on his way home from work or the store,
hardly poor either with all that roadkill to scarf down . . .

So maybe for once I've nailed you, my misery . . .
Short swoop from one hill to the next, and maybe a tango it is . . .
Forget gurgle in dragon, forget Vivaldi . . . Go with the crow!

MASK

Nobody had to tell me in the monster movie to hide my eyes and not look—
  it hurt to be frightened.
You can't not look, though, later on in the movie of mind: that sex theater in-
  side you, that thug.

I'd think: inside I must be an evil person: didn't I lust, wouldn't I be if I could
  that big-bellied thug?
Or was it rather: I must be inside an evil person; these famished eyes, this in-
  satiable staring?

No surprise I'd decide I'd need a mask to live in, a disguise to conceal the
  monster I was certain I was.
Not the Lone Ranger's—I knew that cheap muslin from Halloween: I needed
  a real mask.

No matter Santayana warning: "A mask is not responsive, you must not speak
  to it or kiss it."
No matter Hölderlin's doctor, inventing a mask for his tormented patients so
  they couldn't scream.

Didn't Yeats have his file of fake Willies? His Anti-Self, his Cuchulain, his
  Michael Robartes?
Why couldn't I then? Why was I stranded like the insole of a shoe in this face
  glued on so tightly?

Yet when I'd borrow masks, nothing ever quite fit, and they'd soon become
   shapeless and stink.
Better the semblance, I thought, with no conscience or name, that takes any
   impress, like free verse.

But within that face was silence, then sound, too much of one, then too much
   of the other:
grinding together like gears, they extruded a wobbly, always weirdly wrong
   word-glop.

Years pass. Love, no love. At last arrives Dr. Freud, who opens your face so you
   can look in:
desire, terror, and rage twined writhing together, and "*Id*," consoles Freud,
   "call it your *Id*."

So there you are, the inside of your psyche riven with scar, waiting to heal,
   knit, become true . . .
But hadn't we already died waiting? Weren't we scattered like crumbs through
   the Pleistocene forest

for Hänsel and Gretel to gather and hand on to Marx, who'd proclaim the face
   itself was the veil,
beaten capitalist gold, cunning, entrancing, enchanting, like the death mask
   of Agamemnon?

. . . Old age then, skull in the mirror with jowls and hair in its ears, arriving
   without your permission.
This iron mask, this simulacrum, bland, boring, unsexy, locked to you like a
   chastity belt.

How it barely cracks smiles, how it moons dolefully back at you like your dog,
   how it can't lie.
Old Rocky Face, crumbling, eroding; unmasked lonely ranger, and this time
   no covering your eyes.

WATCHING THE TELLY WITH NIETZSCHE

Sucking up another dumb movie on HBO, it comes to me how boring it is to
 sit here like a boil on an ass.
Boring, not as in Berryman's "Life, friends is boring we must not say so . . ."—
 life isn't boring,
just thinking of matters which don't set my teeth on fire and make the dents
 in my brain screech is boring.

For instance: I switch to a news channel and a segment about what a Repub-
 lican president wannabe—
I refuse to utter his name—proclaimed on being caught changing his cha-
 meleon mind about something:
"*Quoting me is lying about me.*" Now that's not boring, is it? That leaps right
 into your vault, no?

A person denouncing his own convictions as possibly being too true? My god,
 Nietzsche himself
(and he was in my philosophical gawk-time all but my god), who growled of
 our having "gnawed at ourselves,"
and "turned ourselves into torture chambers," wouldn't have known what to
 make of such conscienceless crap . . .

Wait, though, maybe as my mother would say I'm overexcited—I've always
   been such a weep.
That political lizard and those like him—so many like him—are hardly the
   worst things in the world.
Think Stalin. Think Mandelstam on his hell-train, shuddering with fever,
   dying of a line in a poem.

And remember how that Dream Song continues? "After all, the sky flashes,
   the great sea yearns,
we ourselves flash and yearn . . ." and they do, and we do, but we're terrified,
   too, sometimes of,
sometimes for, and sometimes we can't tell the difference, because history
   shudders and Mandlestam dies,

and it can seem only the torturers and tyrants, the venal demagogues and the
   qualmless deceivers
stand firm, gazing out over the hapless rest of us to decide which will be next,
   which Mandlestam,
which flash and which yearning will be dragged down and submerged in their
   political puke . . .

As I'm dragged down into the ocean of cathode image-scum pumping out at
   me from the sewer-screen,
rendering me gloomy beyond gloom, not beyond Berryman's, please, but still,
   my tail is lashing,
fangs are unsheathing in the lining of my heart . . . Better turn it off—all of it,
   off. Jesus Christ, *off*!

EXHAUST

My grandson wants a *Ferrari*. I buy one for him. Why not?
The second a *Mercedes*. The third a *Porsche*. Why not?
How things change — my grandfather wanted only the pickup
one icy Rochester night the year before I was born
he skidded through a gate in and plowed head on into a train.

My grandsons' cars cost a dollar, part of a vast collection
of racers, convertibles, trucks, even antiques from the time
I had my first car, a five-year-old ungainly green *Chevy*,
not like Lowell's father's spanking new one — "with gilded hooves,"
wrote Lowell, and, slashingly, "his best friend."

I treasured my *Chevy*, too, though it plodded compared with
a friend's *Olds* that sped us one New Year's Eve
after the parties down the parkway at a hundred and ten.
My grandfather I gather was vain of his truck, and his driving,
but my grandmother would grumble, "He was a terrible driver."

We were good drivers, we were certain, better than good —
didn't we all but live in our cars? Wasn't the best part even
of a date when you made out with your girlfriend in back?
Right now, hitting *a hundred*, don't we love each other
for how our tires are glued to the pavement and life has no end?

I hadn't seen Warhol's print yet of mangled teenagers
spilled from their wreck. I didn't see much then beyond cars,
like my grandsons, who know every make, model,
top speed and zero to sixty by heart, and who'll squabble
because one has stolen another's X-something or other.

My grandfather was a socialist when that word still could be used.
He even ran for state senate, though not surprisingly lost—
he was hardly well-off, with a store that sold candy and papers,
and why he needed that broken-down truck, my grandmother
still complained on her deathbed, was a mystery to her.

The first time I was almost killed in a car, an axle sheared,
our back wheel bounced past us, we spun out of control
over a busy highway, and pulled up a yard from a tree,
much like the tree in the photo of the death of Camus
with his publisher's sports car gruesomely wrapped around it.

Such a short time between my automobile madness
and my rapture reading Camus—Sisyphus telling me why
suicide wasn't the route, though at the time it could seem so.
What did he say exactly? I don't think there was much about love,
which would be my reason now: love, family, poetry, art.

I sometimes imagined my Chevy was devoted to me, like a dog.
That was before death arrived; mine and everyone else's.
Anne Sexton's father died in a car: dear Anne made certain to, too.
Pollock, Sebald, Nathanael West; Tom Mix, for god's sake;
me nearly four times, and my grandfather Charles Kasdin.

Whom I just realized now I miss, and whom if I'd been there
I know I could have saved: *Pump the brakes gently*, I'd tell him,
and we'd glide up to the rails, and wait in the beautiful snow.
He'd offer some wisdom to hand on to my grandsons,
the train clattering by us, the mingling steam of our breath.

PROSE

I live on prose, I devour prose, I gorge prose till I'm ready to puke, but it's keep-
ing me sane:
these are the miserable months in that miserable Paris hotel in the wretched
blot of being nineteen

when I want to write poems but don't know how to begin, so I stuff prose into
the empty hours
like one of those screaming chipping machines that turn matter to mass, and
I stay more or less sane.

I also read, try to read poems, Eliot, say: I rattle around in *The Waste Land* and
fall on the floor.
Forget tabula rasa, I'm tabula nothing. How could anyone know this little?
What else then but prose?

Sometimes I give up even on it and drag myself out to the streets like Wyatt
in Gaddis's *Recognitions*,
or find myself on a bridge like Quentin in *The Sound and the Fury* but at least
I don't jump.

So maybe the novelists do save me, maybe Lawrence and Mann, Dickens and
Melville and Greene,
even the landslides of Thomas Wolfe that go through me like castor oil release
me from myself.

And Hemingway—*Papa!*—I slug down every word, and imagine I might be
one of his heroes, or him,
the him who could make being impotent or having your lover die sound like
the best thing in the world.

I had no idea it was his prose, the damned *prose*, those soldered declarative
phrases, that stoical syntax
you rode like a long-distance bus, or that he was a shit to his friends, and would
soon do himself in.

How know either, crouched haplessly in myself like an ape in a cage and all
but tearing to pieces,
that in a blink, two blinks, I'd be all the way here, looking back—and it'll be
gone, really gone,

the miles of novels, the tens of thousands of poems, read, written, not writ-
ten . . . Not written . . .
Weren't the books not written what Hemingway died of? And that prose he
could never outgrow?

What have I left unwritten? Never outgrown? One of my grandsons when he
was four said to his mother,
"Next time Baba is little"—Baba is me—"I'm going to read this book to him,
Mama, okay?"

Nice thought, to do it again. Maybe this time the ignorance will seem more
innocence and less curse,
less like climbing Kilimanjaro, and more like finally finishing nursery school,
at least that.

BUTCHERS

1.

Thank goodness we were able to wipe the Neanderthals out, beastly things,
from our mountains, our tundra — that way we had all the meat we might need.

Thus the butcher can display under our eyes his scrubbed hands on the block,
and never refer to the rooms hidden behind where dissections are effected,

where flesh is reduced to its shivering atoms and remade for our delectation
as cubes, cylinders, barely material puddles of admixtured horror and blood.

Rembrandt knew of all this — isn't his flayed beef carcass really a caveman?
It's Christ also, of course, but much more a troglodyte such as we no longer are.

Vanished those species — begone! — those tribes, those peoples, those nations —
Myrmidon, Ottoman, Olmec, Huron, and Kush: gone, gone, and goodbye.

2.

But back to the chamber of torture, to Rembrandt, who was telling us surely
that hoisted with such cables and hung from such hooks we too would reveal

within us intricate layerings of color and pain: alive the brush is with pain,
aglow with the cruelties of crimson, the cooled, oblivious ivory of our innards.

Fling out the hooves of your hands! Open your breast, pluck out like an Aztec
your heart howling its Cro-Magnon cries that compel to battles of riddance!

Our own planet at last, where purged of wilderness, homesickness, prowling,
we're no longer compelled to devour our enemies' brains, thanks to our butcher,

who inhabits this palace, this senate, this sentried barbed-wire enclosure
where dare enter none but subservient breeze; bent, broken blossom; dry rain.

CANCER

Does it really all come down to the woman in the dry cleaner's who by her vo-
　　ciferous silence
and the way she flings them down lets me know she's espied the indelible yel-
　　low driblets

on the lining of my pants and hates me for them, thrusting them with loathing
　　into their plastic
and not looking for an instant at my eyes, my face?—And for this that she
　　won't accept money

directly from my hand, making clear I'm to leave my filthy bill in the dent of
　　the plastic tray,
that the change will be deposited there for my polluted, contagious fingers to
　　extract?

Was it for this, *this*, becoming a *patient*, transformed to a shivering sack of
　　blood to be spilled?
And the dark night tracing of malevolent lymph tracks, fear scaling the ice-
　　rungs of my spine?

For this the surgeon's blade slicing the fat of my gut, leaving that dismal shelf
　　over my groin?
And the pain, the shuddering post-operative chill, the potassium burningly
　　blown into my veins?

. . . But listen to me, complaining: Who cares if some snob-bitch turns up her
    nose at my crotch?
And you, cancer-fiend, still maybe spitting cells out into my bones and my
    brain, fuck you:

fuck you for Zweig, fuck you for Fagles, fuck you for McGrew and Minghella
    and the poets —
Cavafy and both Hugheses, and Ginsberg and Clifton and Jane Kenyon and
    even John Donne,

plus all the big public deals like Bogart and Marley and that Beatle, and also
    the beautiful starlet
who wouldn't let them cut off her perfect breasts and so died of the fear of los-
    ing her beauty.

Too late for me to be frightened of losing my potbellied unbeauty, or anything
    else except maybe things
like remembering when Erv Goffman was dying and I said, "What will I do
    with only one superego?"

and he laughed, and I laughed, and what can you do, with everyone plucked
    out of your life except laugh?
Or not laugh, not every day, but not cry either, or maybe a little, maybe cry
    just a little, a little.

WALL

Snarling, stinking, snapping his fore-fangs,
out of the woods, wild waste beyond woods,
comes beast, comes brute, carnivorous, ravenous,
but before him—and oh, we were saved—rose our wall.

Violent, fearsome, with invulnerable helmet and shield,
comes antagonist, foe, furious, pitiless, lethal,
axmen behind him chanting their cuneiform curse,
but before him—and, oh, saved again—loomed our wall.

So we raised ever more walls, even walls
that might fail: Jericho shucked from its ramparts,
men, women, old, young, all slaughtered.
What did it matter? We believed still in our wall.

Then the inspiration to build walls facing in!
Reservation, concentration camp, ghetto,
finally whole countries walled in, and saved were we
from traitors who'd dare wish to flee our within.

That such walls fail, too, fall, too? No matter.
Only raise more. That all walls, facing out or in,
fail, fall, leaving fossils of lives in numb rubble?
No matter. Raise more. Only raise more.

CRAZY

Wordsworth has crawled from his cradle to Hölderlin's cradle to murmur in
  Hölderlin's ear.
Wordsworth's two weeks younger, but much farther advanced en route to the
  cruelties of art.

"Now believing," he intones, "now disbelieving . . ." the nipple pops from
  Hölderlin's lips,
and Wordsworth, gleeful, continues: ". . . perplexed with impulse, motive,
  right and wrong . . ."

"Wrong," Hölderlin hears, stricken with realizing he should have stayed in
  the womb,
and, "Wrong," begins his first poem, the one he won't write—Don't write! he
  sobs, already half mad.

I'm sobbing too nearly, because I can't begin to fathom the glory of Hölder-
  lin's wild singing,
his "Gods Walking," his "Patmos"—I was on Patmos, he never was, but I'll
  never know his sublime isle.

Because I can't read German, and Hölderlin's genius isn't there, except in his
  original tongue.
And neither is Schiller's nor Goethe's . . . Tsvetaeva, Mandelstam, Pindar, the
  Dark Age Arabs and Jews.

Even gigantic Pushkin, though Nabokov dragged him over the cobbles to
Nabokovian English . . .
Nobody's there, it feels like, except Wordsworth, who drones mournfully into
the cradle of my age.

He wants me to be not like Hölderlin, silent and wise and insane, but the way
he himself was at the end,
stodgy, staid, spitting up the pabulum drool of his dotage, the fires out, the
passion quenched.

And how avoid that worse-than-death doom when to help me are only the li-
brary of poems
I've devoured in English and French and the few others that make it across
the language abyss?

Hymn to me, Hölderlin! Just tracing the words on the page I can tell how high
is your flight!
Save me from my sublunary trudge, this monolingual Ferris wheel to which
I'm condemned!

Let us be crazy together! Don't leave me scrambling up those stanzas of in-
accessible bliss!
Helfen Sie mir! or something. Something in Mandelstam's Russian. Some
baby babble. Some soar.

THE INVISIBLE NUNS,
SISTER JOHN, AND THE SAINT

Upstream the village house convent in which they invisibly dwell;
near us, a stink, fetid and foul: their cesspool's overflowed,
the ancient waste seeps down the innocent brook onto the fields.

What is it to live in the ever-closed convent, invisible in the stink?
"Eternally dark, eternally rank, gloomy, gorgeous," says the Saint—
"Regard the gold glowing limestone, tile roofs, iris-topped walls."

Ablutions, purifications, gentle scrubbings under the habit.
Yet, *"Full of wailing, complaining, and sharp, fierce crying,"*
the Saint avers would be their psyches untempered by confinement.

And the radical nun Sister John we knew once? Is she there?
Who in the long-ago days of the pre-conservative popes lived in the slums,
riding the subway in sweater and jeans to minister to the poor?

Has Sister John, too, been compelled behind gold glowing walls?
Do she and her sisters still hear in their cells the subway's despair?
"Despair, despair," cry the sharp steel wheels, *"Woe, woe,"* cry the nuns,

while *"Renounce,"* the Saint commands, *"the dismal, grim world,"*
though Sister John surely would bless the flow of shit and debris,
and curse the crimes perpetrated against the helpless and needy as vile.

"*Venomous, poisonous, endlessly hateful*," the Saint howls again,
with his voice, his breath, his strength, his poison, his wrath,
as he sails in his wave-beaten, wave-bitten barque in search

of the Isle of True Faith, where none dwell, as well knows Sister John,
not the "*everlastingly chaste*," nor the "*silken and silver garbed rich*."
"*Only*," she'd cry and accuse, "*the dark, dire divine of the slum*."

HASTE

Not so fast people were always telling me *Slow down take your time* teachers
    coaches
the guy who taught me to ride ("*Stop cowboying*" he'd shout as if that wasn't
    the point)

but the admonition that stuck was the whisper that girl that woman that
    smudged now
dear girl-woman legs so tightly wound round me sighed young as she was to
    my ear

Ah the celestial contraption we made though—no matter how you swerved
    it it held together
Why not go faster? But she with her fluttery guttural *Slower go slower* knew
    better knew better

No one says *Not so fast* now not Catherine when I hold her not our dog as I
    putter behind her
yet everything past present future rushes so quickly through me I've frayed
    like a flag

Unbuckle your spurs life don't you know up ahead where the road ends there's
    an abyss?
No room for galloping anymore here Surely by now you should know better
    know better

TIMELINE

Count they teach me so I count I count to ten I count to a hundred a thousand
then I'm taught math I add subtract multiply just as I'm told but they never
    let on
I'd still now be obsessively trying to calculate how to make things make sense

I've lived for instance as of today twenty-six thousand nine hundred ten days
as long as Sidney and Burns put together Plath and Purcell Crane plus Mozart
plus a few thousand sad for them but for me it all slides away into the seethe

Eight years it took between grasping there was this mind-thing in my head
and King's vision and the war when my conscience began throwing its tantrums
and what have I managed to do with the five hundred and sixty months since?

My life's a topological monster not enough room in the century I was born in
too much in the one where I'll die so many blots and erasures maybe I'll
    borrow
some other century to better graph my trajectory a good one say the nineteenth

In twenty—let's see—six it would be to end at the end Jefferson dies and Adams
the year before Blake then my crazily fortunate span later in nineteen aught
    zero
come Einstein's theory and Planck's Freud's *Dreams* Kodak cameras and cars

Between all in the length of my sprawl amazing Keats born and dead likewise
Van Gogh Whitman Nietzsche and Marx there's Gettysburg Wounded Knee
the futile revolutions this war that war and wait I've consumed a lifetime again

And here I am my own extinction in sight and everything still such a screwup
the old immoralities and injustice plus our dear world so wounded "Give me
    a fear"
prayed Donne "of which I may not be afraid" but my fears square cube
    quadruple

If you could only cipher back to that day in first grade before numbers and
    start
over kindly Miss Watson commanding "Don't count on your fingers" but
    this time
though you cross your heart that you won't you do eight nine ten damn it
    you do

Black coal with a thunderous shush plunging down the chute into its clearly
   evil inhabited coal bin.
The black furnace in whose frightening maw you'd feed paper to watch it curl
   to black char.

The incomprehensible marks on blackboards at school you conquered with-
   out knowing quite how.
The black ink in the inkwell in your desk, the metal pens with blots that dia-
   bolically slid from their nibs.

The hats women sported with black, mysterious veils, even your mother; the
   "mascara" she'd apply
more meticulously than she did anything else — with her black lashes she was
   almost somebody else.

Black slush after the blizzard had passed and the diesel buses and trucks were
   fuming again,
but you still remembered how blackly vividly lovely the branches of trees
   looked in new snow.

The gunk on the chain of your bike then on your pants leg, the black stuff al-
   ways under your nails.
Where did it come from, how get it out? Even between your toes sometimes
   there was black.

The filthy tires hung on hooks in the garage-store we had to pass through to
  get to our minuscule *shul*.
Black Book of Europe, proof of the war on the Jews — illicit volume, as forbid-
  den to Jewish children as porn.

Black people the states in the South began to send up, keeping what they
  needed for cheap labor and maids
and exporting the rest: a stream of discarded humans, with the manufactur-
  ing plants just closing down.

The photo of black children in the twenties, frolicking on the bench of the
  Lincoln statue by the courthouse.
I took the bus once to go sit in its lap, *his* lap — how kind he looked, how sur-
  prisingly hard the bronze lap.

Another statue, *Captive's Choice*, in a park: the girl kidnapped by Indians who
  forgets she's white,
then, "saved," gives up Indian husband and children. Who decided it should
  have been that, and there?

The first black kids in our school, fine with me, because Clarence Murphy,
  fifteen in fourth grade,
stopping beating me up because I'd killed Christ and raged instead with even
  more venom at them.

I was afraid of Clarence but not of black people, except that day on the bus:
  the sweat-stench of men
who'd worked hard and not had time yet to change. Though I already knew it
  was shameful, I fled.

"Blackballs" to keep Jews, Italians, Irish, then blacks out of the clubs in
   Maplewood and Montclair.
The unfunny jokes about the mythical signs on their gates: *No Dogs, Niggers,*
   and Especially Jews.

Our gangster hero, Longie Zwillman, who had a black car; so did our may-
   ors—bought off by "interests."
Jewish, Irish, Italian, then at last a black mayor: the owned ones with their
   Cadillacs of corruption.

Thick soot on the bricks of the mills by the tracks, smoke darkly billowing,
   then extinguished forever.
Rivers with rainbows of oil on their lids, their beds eternally black venomous
   chemical sludge.

Miles of black turnpike and parkway pavement scrolled out onto the soil of
   the no-longer farms;
you could speed from exit to exit and not notice the city slums, the factories
   in broken-eyed ruin.

Shopping malls, suburbs, urban flight, urban decay; downtown the depart-
   ment stores shuttered, gutted,
then small businesses, theaters, the rest. Everywhere desolation, did no one
   see it approaching?

The finally hardly recognizable city; storms of dereliction, of evasion, had all
   but swept it away.
A place of ghosts; only the people, left to struggle, left to cope, and Lincoln
   on his lonely bench, still real.

THE MUSE GENE

My Australopithecus-self dumbfoundedly watches
my muse-self pirouette in a pigsty and spill,
those unblemished legs flung every which way,
those bounteous breasts flopped like the dugs of a dog.

He tries, innocent thing, not to see, to have seen.
To evolve all this way and have beauty be ugly?
Is this what's meant by the "modern"?
It's worse than our old life as prey.

. . . And, really, was the savannah so bad? Predators,
yes, but no TV, no malls. To eat: yum,
berries and bugs; medium cyclic sex drive.
Who needed a stunt-flying klutz of a muse?

Consider her point of view, though: that meagerly
minded ape-person can't even revise.
Imagine: life as first draft—up the hill, draft;
down the hill, draft—draft, draft, draft.

No wonder muse-self would lose interest.
No wonder wander. Live with a one-psychèd brute?
No wonder my room stinks like a sweatshop.
No wonder headaches, no wonder blank.

Maybe it wasn't a great idea nailing wings
to such a recalcitrant screech.
But what a good time we've had *à trois*.
Up the hill, down the hill: forward march!

LA CHATTE

Colette's heroine's so sexually neglected she pushes her husband's cat—
pussy, dear puss—off the balcony of his rich family apartment.
Pussy lands, saved, on an awning. Doorman brings her back up. Pity.

It's some Tibetan who rhapsodized, "The body's a shout," not Colette,
but she could have. In Paris they say that when she made love
she'd sometimes cry out with such abandon her neighbors applauded.

My body, too, all but shouted when Catherine came last night to bed—
she moved with a muscular, athletic sweep I hadn't registered before,
that engendered a *gust* in me such that I felt I'd never made love,

with her or anyone else until now, and afterwards—afterwards, oh—
it was still there, the gust, I'd become merely it seemed its container,
and Catherine was still there, in the grace of her falling asleep,

and it came to me to take her body into my mouth, her whole body,
thighs, buttocks, slim waist, breasts, skull busily buzzing—
all of it, grace notes, arpeggios, trills, and yes, pussy, dear puss,

and roll it on my tongue, inside my cheeks to the roof of my mouth . . .
And if she could really be in there, I wonder what she would feel?
A sweet lollipop river, I'd like to think; no rapids, only the gentlest

rolling and pitching—lifted she'd be, and let fall and lifted again,
not fall and lifted like that cursed cat carried back purring
to the husband who deserved the celibacy he was surely condemned to,

but lifted as Colette was those mythical evenings in her opera of sex,
and as my gust, of desire, of longing, of love, was loosed and lifted in me,
wildly lashing the branches, joyously twirling the leaves.

SPEW

1.

Auden awed, Auden actually awed, by another poet's intelligence, in an essay
    on Marianne Moore,
and as much by her skill as, in a poem about a pelican, the "elaborate reversed
    epic simile" he notes
she devises, in which, sliding a para-rhyme from *Hänsel,* she reveals details of
    the life of *Handel.*

What would Moore have written—assembled and welded might be the
    term—about the pelican,
slimed in gulf oil, helpless as a just-born mammal but hideously unlicked,
    I watch on the news, dying,
then dead, whose corpse a volunteer holds before her like the Virgin her
    Christ child and cries?

2.

Hopkins—Auden admired him, too—threatened his own eye made with a
    "prick . . . no eye at all"
to have to behold *"only ten or twelve"* Binsey poplars felled: what would he
    wreak to witness
shores slathered with pitch, creatures small and large smothered, the sea with
    a crust of black scab?

Battling despair, Hopkins perhaps spoke of ours, and of us: ". . . *their packs*
   infest the age."
"*After-comers,"* he called us, who'd never guess "*the beauty been,"* and will our
   own afters believe
how we hid our eyes like Masaccio's miserable Adam as we slunk from our
   Eden, for this was our Eden?

3.

Auden mourned the vanishing "*mass and majesty of this world,"* and Moore
   foresaw "*the tired*
moment of danger that lays on the heart and lungs the / weight of the python
   that crushes to powder . . ."
"*Manwolf,"* Hopkins calls us, and "*mortal trash,"* ". . . *whose strokes of havoc*
   unselve . . . us."

On the screen, in her befouled industrial gloves, the young woman still sobs.
   "*If I do well"*—
Moore once more—"*I am blessed / whether any bless me or not, and if I do*
   ill / I am cursed."
And if I do naught? . . . Moore's pelican "*wastes the moon"*—"*O pity and*
   indignation"—we waste world.

STATIONS

"Seule la rose
est assez fragile
pour exprimer
l'Eternité . . ."

by Paul Claudel is this month's poster poem on the Métro,
and, Paul Claudel, I think, wouldn't you know it?—
"Only the rose is fragile enough to express Eternity . . ."
What does "rose" have to do with anything really?
"Red rose, proud rose . . ."—second-rate, juvenile Yeats.
Even Rilke: that "rose of pure contradiction"
was hardly Rainer at his best. Hell, why not *"heart"*?
"Only the human heart, is vulnerable enough . . ."

We're in a station now, *Strasbourg–Saint-Denis,*
where young immigrants sell hash, and—so stupid—
crack cocaine, and thinking about it sets me brooding
whether France is becoming too much like home.
". . . Only the social contract is precarious enough . . ."
but thank goodness the doors of my car are closing
because a fierce-looking guy was glaring from the quai
the way it happens in New York though still rarely here.

Next *Etienne Marcel*, a billboard for an AIDS group,
spouses, parents, sad offspring of the afflicted . . .
"Only the illusion of well-being is tenuous enough . . ."
then *Les Halles*, where teens from the *banlieues* hang out,
and, if the place were picturesque, you'd say *"promenade"*
and where I watch a honey-hued, truly ravishing
young woman stalk away from a forlorn younger man—
"Only the pain of a boy scorned by a goddess-like girl . . ."

Overstatement? Rose with thorn? Who cares?
Châtelet now, and I'm beginning to weary of this,
start to think "rose" might after all not be so bad
when there's so much to account for.
"Only the rose can stand for . . ." No, dumb.
Symbolize? Manifest? Embody? . . . Stop!
End of the line. Everyone up the stairs and goodbye.
Wait, rose, not you. You, *ma belle rose*, stay here.

POEM FOR MYSELF FOR MY BIRTHDAY

It's coming at me again, damn, like that elephant with its schoonering ears
   charging in Uganda.
We were okay, we thought, in our Rover, so it was a nice mix of scary and
   thrilling, plus a story to tell—
that behemoth, Wow! snorting a few yards off in the bush, waving his huge
   crushing tusks.

Then rushing out at us. At us. Like my birthday. Like thinking of birthdays,
   this one, the next,
the next to last and—ouch—the last, all stampeding towards me like that
   most likely ill outlaw,
ponderous-looking but so fast on his feet you can't even dream of dancing out
   of the way.

Out of the way! Step on the gas! Okay, we're out of there, safe! . . . Wait,
   though, I'm not safe,
this time my birthday's a tractor trailer skidding sideways on ice and I'm
   noodling by on my bike,
my darling old Raleigh, and the whole frame's pretzeled around me. Happy
   birthday? Oh, please.

My last happy was that first one with a party—gooey brown cake and four
　　beautiful candles.
And they're singing, to me! Even now it seems worth having lost one of my
　　not-enough years.
I loved being sung to. And how not love that song? Especially "... to you!" To
　　be "you" in a song!

Now I'm often "you" to myself. You selfish bastard, you indolent slug. When
　　did that happen?
I see the Dalai Lama's birthday's here, too; in his photo, he pumps a treadmill
　　like a prayer wheel,
and proclaims (boasts? admits?), "I visualize my death every day." I wonder if
　　he's "you" to himself?

Speaking of visualization: Yash Glatshteyn has a poem, "For My Two Hun-
　　dredth Birthday,"
where he "talks of words" with friends in the garden, then makes love to his
　　"soft, obedient maid."
Very sweet, nostalgia for the future, ingenious device when your present's all
　　but used up.

But forget the meshugeneh future, I can't even get the past straight: every-
　　thing keeps popping up changed.
It's like being, not being in, *being*, one of those movies that starts with a flash
　　forward, then—poof!—
the plot's rushed ahead and you're still back where you began and way out
　　here near the end.

Did Glatshteyn's wife ever forgive him that succulent poem-maid? Catherine
would go crazy.

No problem for the celibate Dalai Lama, though I'd bet there've been enough
"maids" he could have . . .

Well, slept with, the way Gandhi slept with young girls when he was old—to
keep warm, he avowed.

As did King David. All those thank-you notes to be written, those apology
calls. You liar. You cheat.

Happy Birthday to me. Dalai Lama and me. By now that poor stricken ele-
phant's probably dead.

To him, too, Happy Returns. And me, spinning by on my bike, singing, "To
you; oh, to you."

DRAFT 23

East, vast American flag Whitman sunrise; west, Jeffers' roan searchlight scissoring the dusk;
between, squads platoons divisions of poets scribbling slashing revising correcting rejecting . . .
What scribble are we trying to do? What have we done? What imagine slash when we began this?

North, geometrical Frostian ice storms; south, Neruda-diamonds scorching the cordilleras.
The voice dulls balks desires only to give itself over as it once seemed to to the swells surges concussions;
not this compulsion to retune the unmalleable self-music even in bliss we're condemned to.

That way, Roethke's "washed-out interrupted raw places"; this, Eliot's "fragments I have shored . . ."
Between we scribble and slash — are we trying to change the world by changing the words?
Delete malice oppression tyranny poverty cruelty by our rage our raging obsession to amend?

Innocent scribble innocent slash who more credulous than we who more rendingly harmless?

Are there songs of the soul yet unsung to calm our doubt and despair? Will we have to revise them?

"*O cut the sweet apple and share it* . . ." Sweet scribble sweet slash O write the poem sweetly and share it.

SALT

Abashingly eerie that just because I'm here on the long low-tide beach of age
    with briny time
licking insidious eddies over my toes there'd rise in me those mad weeks a life-
    time ago
when I had two lovers, one who soaked herself so in *Chanel* that before I went
    to the other
I'd scrub with fistfuls of salt and not only would the stink be vanquished but
    I'd feel shame-shriven, pure,
which thinking about is a joke: how not acknowledge—obsolete notion or
    no—that I was a *cad*.

Luckily though, I've hung onto my Cornell box of pastness with its ten thou-
    sand compartments,
so there's a place for these miniature mountains of salt, each with its code-tag
    of amnesia,
and also for the flock of Donnas and Ednas and Annies, a resplendent feather
    from each,
and though they're from the times I was not only crass, stupid, and selfish but
    thoughtless—
art word for shitty—their beaks open now not to berate but stereophonically
    warble forgiveness.

Such an engrossing contrivance: up near a corner, in tinsel, my memory
    moon, still glowing,
still cruel, because of the misery it magnified the times *I* was abandoned—
    "They flee . . . oh they flee . . ."
I'd abrade myself then not with salt but anapests, iambs, enjambments, and
    here they still are,
burned in in ink, but here too, dead center, Catherine, with her hand-carved
    frame in a frame—
like the hero in Westerns who arrives just in time to rescue the town she gal-
    loped up to save me.

Well, I suppose soon the lid with its unpickable latch will come down, but the
    top I hope will be glass,
see-through, like Cornell's, so I'll watch myself for a while boinging around
    like a pinball,
still loving this flipper-thing life that so surprisingly cannoned me up from
    oblivion's ramp,
and to which I learned to sing in my own voice but sometimes thanks be in
    the voice of others,
which is why I can croon now, "My lute be still . . ." and why I can cry,
    ". . . for I have done."

THE DAY CONTINUES LOVELY

With *Fear and Trembling* I studied my Kierkegaard, with *Sickness unto Death*
I contemplated with him my spiritual shortcomings, and it didn't occur to me
until now that in the Kierkegaard I've read he never takes time to actually pray.
Odd . . . This isn't to question his faith—who'd dare?—but his . . . well, agenda.
All those intricate paradoxes of belief he devotes his time to untying, retying.
Can it be that Kierkegaard simply *forgets* to pray, he's so busy untying, retying?
I understand that: I have times I forget to remember I can't pray. *Can't. Pray.*

This June morning just after sparkling daybreak and here I'm not praying.
My three grandsons asleep on their mats on the floor of my study,
shining, all three, more golden than gold, and I'm still not. *Not praying.*
Why aren't I? Even our dog Bwindi sprawled beside Turner, the youngest,
Turner's sleep-curled fist on her back: Why haven't I prayed about them?
I can imagine someday something inside me saying: *Well, why don't you?*
Something inside me. As though suddenly would be *something inside me.*

There's a Buber story I'm probably misrepresenting that touches on this.
A rabbi spends endless hours deciding whether to do good deeds or pray.
He thinks this first, then that: *This might be good; maybe that would be better,*
and suddenly a VOICE that can only be God's erupts: *STOP DAWDLING!*
And *God*, he thinks: he's been chastised by *God*. *STOP DAWDLING!*
And what happens then? In my anti-Bubering of the tale, everything's lost,
the fool's had his moment with God—even Moses had only how many?—

and he's squandered it because all he could do was stand stunned,
mouth hung metaphorically open, losing his chance to ask for guidance,
but he'd vacillated again and *What happens now?* he wonders in anguish.
Maybe I should get out of this business, find a teaching job, write a book,
on my desolation, my suffering, then he hears again, louder, *STOP! STOP!*
but this time it's his own voice, hopelessly loud, and he knows he'll forever be
in this waiting, this without-God, his glimpse of the Undeniable already waning.

And what about me? Leave aside Kierkegaard, Buber, the rabbis — just me.
Haven't I spent my life trying to make up my mind about *something*?
God, not God; soul, not soul. I'm like the Binary Kid: on, off; off, on.
But isn't that what we all are? Overgrown electrical circuits? Good, bad.
Hate, love. We go crazy trying to gap the space between on and off,
but there is none. Click. Click. Left: Right. Humans kill one another
because there's no room to maneuver inside those minuscule switches.

Meanwhile cosmos roars with so many voices we can't hear ourselves think.
Galaxy on. Galaxy off. Universe on, but another just behind this one,
one more out front waiting for us to be done. They're flowing across us,
sweet swamps of being — and we thrash in them, waving our futile antennae.
. . . Turner's awake now. He smiles, stands; Bwindi yawns and stands, too.
They come to see what I'm doing. Turner leans his head on my shoulder to peek.
What *am* I doing? Thinking of Kierkegaard. Thinking of beauty. Thinking of
  prayer.

WRITERS WRITING DYING

Many I could name but won't who'd have been furious to die while they were
    sleeping but did—
outrageous, they'd have lamented, and never forgiven the death they'd con-
    strued for themselves
being stolen from them so rudely, so crudely, without feeling themselves like
    rubber gloves
stickily stripped from the innermostness they'd contrived to hoard for so
    long—all of it gone,
squandered, wasted, on what? *Death*, crashingly boring as long as you're able
    to think and write it.

Think, write, write, think: just keep running faster and you won't even notice
    you're dead.
The hard thing's when you're not thinking or writing and as far as you know
    you *are* dead
or might as well be, with no word for yourself, just that suction-shush like a
    heart pump or straw
in a milk shake and death which once wanted only to be sung back to sleep
    with its tired old fangs
has me in its mouth!—and where the hell are you that chunk of dying we used
    to call Muse?

Well, dead or not, at least there was that fancy, of some scribbler, some think-
and-write person,
maybe it was yourself, soaring in the sidereal void, and not only that, you were
holding a banjo
and gleefully strumming, and singing, jaw swung a bit under and off to the
side the way crazily
happily people will do it—singing songs or not even songs, just lolly-molly syl-
lable sounds
and you'd escaped even from language, from having to gab, from having to
write down the idiot gab.

But in the meantime isn't this what it is to be dead, with that Emily-fly
buzzing over your snout
that you're singing almost as she did; so what matter if you died in your sleep
or rushed towards dying
like the Sylvia-Hart part of the tribe who ceased too quickly to be and left out
some stanzas?
You're still aloft with your banjoless banjo, and if you're dead or asleep who
really cares?
Such fun to wake up though! Such fun too if you don't! Keep dying! Keep
writing it down!

ACKNOWLEDGMENTS

Grateful acknowledgment is made to the editors of the following publications, where these poems originally appeared:

Agni: "A Hundred Bones"
The Cortland Review: "Cancer," "Lonely Crow," "The Muse Gene" (originally published as "Ancestors"), "Prose," "Spew"
Granta: "Bianca Burning"
Little Star: "La Chatte"
The Massachusetts Review: "Whacked"
The New York Times: "Wall"
The New Yorker: "Exhaust," "Haste," "Rat Wheel, Dementia, Mont Saint-Michel," "Salt"
Ploughshares: "Timeline"
Poetry: "Butchers"
Poetry London: "Crazy"
PN Review: "La Chatte," "A Hundred Bones," "Mask," "Whacked"
Provincetown Review: "Draft 23"
Salmagundi: "Mask"
Slate: "Watching the Telly with Nietzsche"
The Threepenny Review: "Vile Jelly," "Writers Writing Dying"
Tikkun: "The Day Continues Lovely," "Poem for Myself for My Birthday"

"Newark Noir" was originally published as "Newark Black: 1940–1954" in *New Jersey Noir*, published by Akashic Books, 2011.